Sticker & Quiz Atlas of Britain

Stephanie Turnbull

Designed by Doriana Berkovic and Sam Chandler

Illustrated by Colin King

Additional illustrations by
Stuart Trotter and Non Figg

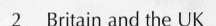

Britain and the UK

Britain is the largest island in Europe. It is made up of three countries: England, Scotland and Wales. Britain and Northern Ireland are together known as the United Kingdom (UK). The rest of Ireland and the Isle of Man are not part of the UK.

Internet links

For links to websites where you can find out lots of amazing facts about Britain and Northern Ireland, go to www.usborne-quicklinks.com

Shetland Islands

Western Isles

Orkney Islands

NORTH SEA

SCOTLAND

ATLANTIC OCEAN

EDINBURGH

NORTHERN IRELAND

BELFAST

Isle of Man

IRISH SEA

REPUBLIC OF IRELAND

ENGLAND

WALES

CARDIFF

LONDON

This map shows Britain, Northern Ireland and other small islands that are part of the United Kingdom. Each country's capital is marked.

Isles of Scilly

ENGLISH CHANNEL

UK flags

The flags of England, Scotland and Ireland combine to form the flag of the UK. This is called the Union Flag, but is usually known as the Union Jack. Wales had already united with England when the first Union Jack was created, in 1606, so the Welsh flag isn't included in the design. The St. Patrick's Cross was included when Ireland became part of the United Kingdom in 1801, and still represents Northern Ireland.

The Union Flag

St. George's Cross of England

The Red Dragon of Wales

St. Andrew's Cross of Scotland

St. Patrick's Cross of Ireland

People and language

There are over 60 million people living in the UK. The main language is English, although Scotland, Wales and Ireland have their own languages too. Many people from other parts of the world have also settled in Britain.

Governments

The UK is run by an elected government, led by the Prime Minister, and the Queen is the head of state. Wales, Northern Ireland and Scotland also have their own governments, which help to run each country.

This is the Saint Edward's Crown, which is worn at the coronation of new kings and queens.

Locator maps

The maps on pages 4–29 each have a small locator map of the UK next to them. The red part tells you which area is shown on the large map.

This locator map goes with the large map of East Anglia.

How to use this book

The stickers in this book show some of the UK's most famous sights and events, including castles, museums, theme parks, sports and festivals. To find out where the stickers go, match them to the black and white outlines on the maps. You can check what the stickers show by finding their matching numbers on the lists next to the maps. There's also a full list of stickers and their page numbers at the back of the book to help you.

London

London is the capital city of England. Around nine million people live there, making it Europe's largest city. It has all kinds of museums and galleries, as well as many large parks. This map shows the middle of the city, where many museums and shops are found.

Internet links
For links to websites where you can find out more about London, go to
www.usborne-quicklinks.com

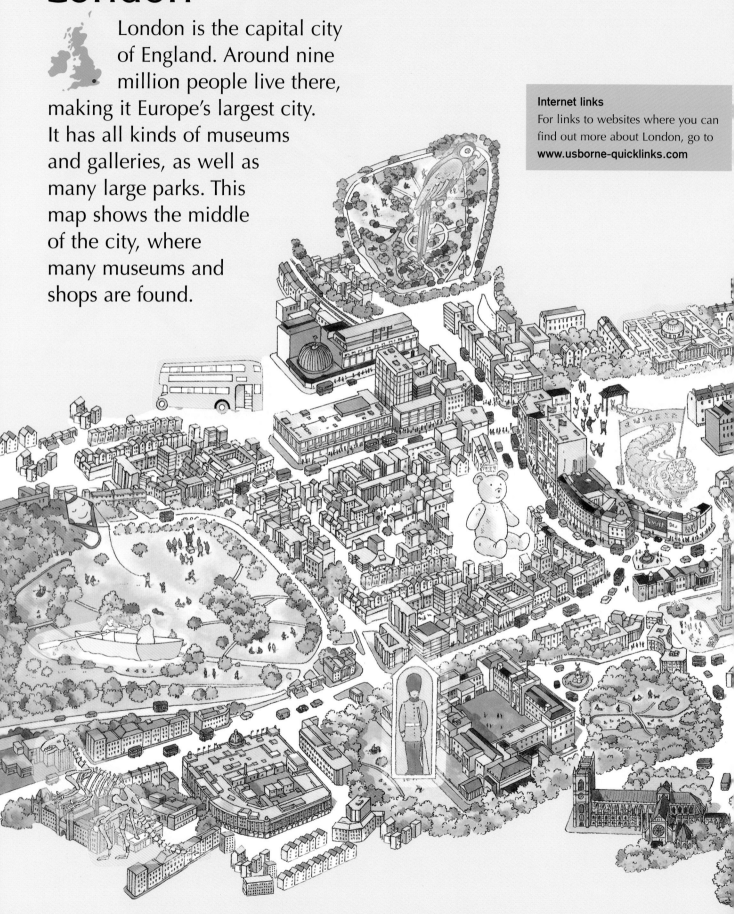

Dinosaur display

The Natural History Museum is one of the largest museums in Europe. It is famous for its spectacular dinosaur exhibits, which include lifelike moving models and a 26m (85ft) long Diplodocus skeleton.

Chinatown

Chinatown is a small part of central London that has become one of the capital's main tourist attractions. Its streets are lined with Chinese restaurants, and every year local Chinese people have a big parade to celebrate Chinese New Year.

London stickers

1 Tower of London
2 Shakespeare's Globe
3 British Museum
4 Clock tower, Houses of Parliament
5 Guard, Buckingham Palace
6 London Eye
7 Hamleys toy store
8 St. Paul's Cathedral
9 Nelson's Column
10 Dinosaur, Natural History Museum
11 Tower Bridge
12 Parrot, London Zoo
13 HMS Belfast
14 Boating, Hyde Park
15 London bus
16 Chinese New Year parade

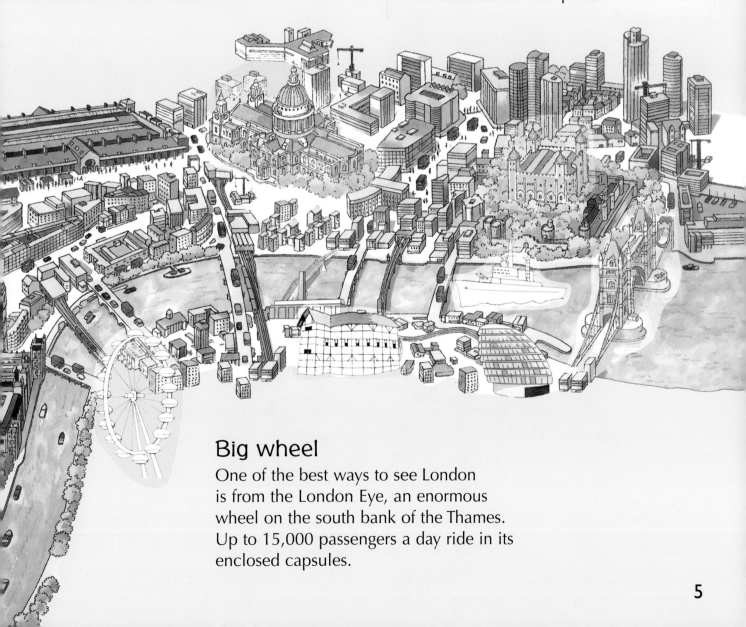

Big wheel

One of the best ways to see London is from the London Eye, an enormous wheel on the south bank of the Thames. Up to 15,000 passengers a day ride in its enclosed capsules.

The West Country

The southwestern corner of England is known as the West Country. It has sandy beaches along the coast, and lush fields and high moors further inland. The West Country is often warmer and sunnier than the rest of Britain.

Rocky ruins

Tintagel Castle stands high on a cliff top beside the Atlantic Ocean. The castle was built in the thirteenth century and is now in ruins. Many people believe that King Arthur, a legendary British ruler in ancient times, was born in an older castle on the same spot.

Giant domes

The Eden Project, in Cornwall, consists of two sets of linked domes that form two huge greenhouses. Different climates from around the world are recreated inside the greenhouses, so that thousands of amazing plants are able to grow there.

Lundy Island

Barnsta Bideford

Hartland Point

ATLANTIC OCEAN

Bude

Bodmin M

Newquay

St. Austell

Whitsand

Redruth

Truro

Falmouth

Penzance

Land's End

Mount's Bay

Isles of Scilly

Lizard Point

Internet links

For links to websites where you can find out more about this region, go to
www.usborne-quicklinks.com

BRISTOL CHANNEL

Mendip Hills

Bridgwater Bay

Bridgwater

Exmoor

Barnstaple

Yeovil

Dartmoor

Exeter

Lyme Bay

Exmouth

Torquay

Plymouth

Start Point

West Country stickers

17	Beach, Torquay
18	Somerset apples
19	Tintagel Castle
20	Bedruthan Steps
21	Poldark Tin Mine
22	Tropical garden, Tresco
23	Deer, Exmoor National Park
24	Exeter Cathedral
25	St. Michael's Mount
26	Ponies, Dartmoor
27	Surfing, Atlantic Ocean
28	Wookey Hole Caves
29	Ottery St. Mary fire festival
30	Eden Project
31	Glastonbury Abbey

Fiery festival

The town of Ottery St. Mary holds an unusual festival on November 5th each year. Local men run through the streets, carrying barrels of burning tar. When the barrels are too hot to hold, they are rolled along the ground until they fall apart.

The South Coast

Along England's south coast are many wide beaches, steep white cliffs and popular seaside resorts. Most visitors to Britain arrive at London's airports, the south coast's busy sea ports, or come via the Channel Tunnel rail link.

Yacht races

Every August, hundreds of yachts from all over the world take part in boat races in the sea around the Isle of Wight. The eight-day event is known as Cowes Week.

Andover
Basingstoke
Hampshire Downs
Winchester
Cranborne Chase
New Forest
North Dorset Downs
Southampton
Portsmouth
Bournemouth
Poole
The Solent
Lyme Bay
South Dorset Downs
Newport
Isle of Wight
Chesil Beach
Weymouth
The Needles
Isle of Portland
Bill of Portland
St. Catherine's Point

Cricket champions

In the 1750s, one of England's most famous cricket clubs was formed in the village of Hambledon. The team became very successful and they recorded many of the rules that are still used. The game of cricket might have started as far back as the 1200s.

City by the sea

Brighton is a lively seaside town. It has a long pier, crammed with amusement arcades and souvenir stalls. Another famous landmark is the Royal Pavilion, a huge white building that is designed to look like an Indian palace.

LONDON

Gravesend

Croydon

Reigate

dford

North Downs

Maidstone

Royal
Tunbridge Wells

rsham

South Downs

Worthing Brighton

Eastbourne

Newhaven

Beachy Head

River Thames

Margate

Canterbury

Ashford

Dover

Folkestone

Dungeness

ENGLISH CHANNEL

North Foreland

Hastings

South Coast stickers

32	National Motor Museum, Beaulieu
33	Cricket match, Hambledon
34	Chessington World of Adventures
35	Drusillas Park, Alfriston
36	Dover Castle
37	HMS Victory, Portsmouth
38	Royal Pavilion, Brighton
39	Channel Tunnel
40	Maiden Castle hill fort, Dorchester
41	Gatwick Airport
42	Canterbury Cathedral
43	Yachting, near the Isle of Wight
44	Leeds Castle
45	Bluebell Railway, near East Grinstead
46	Farnborough International air show
47	Olympic Stadium, London

Underwater trains

The Channel Tunnel is the world's longest undersea rail link. It lies under the English Channel and connects Britain and France. Fast passenger trains take just 21 minutes to travel from one end to the other.

The Heart of England

The central part of England contains
historic houses and mysterious ancient sites.
There is also beautiful countryside, such as
the Chilterns, with their rolling chalk hills, and the
Cotswolds, which are dotted with pretty villages.

Amazing maze

Longleat House, in Wiltshire, is
an Elizabethan mansion that is
open to the public. The gardens
around it contain a safari park
and a massive hedge maze,
made up of more than
16,000 yew trees.

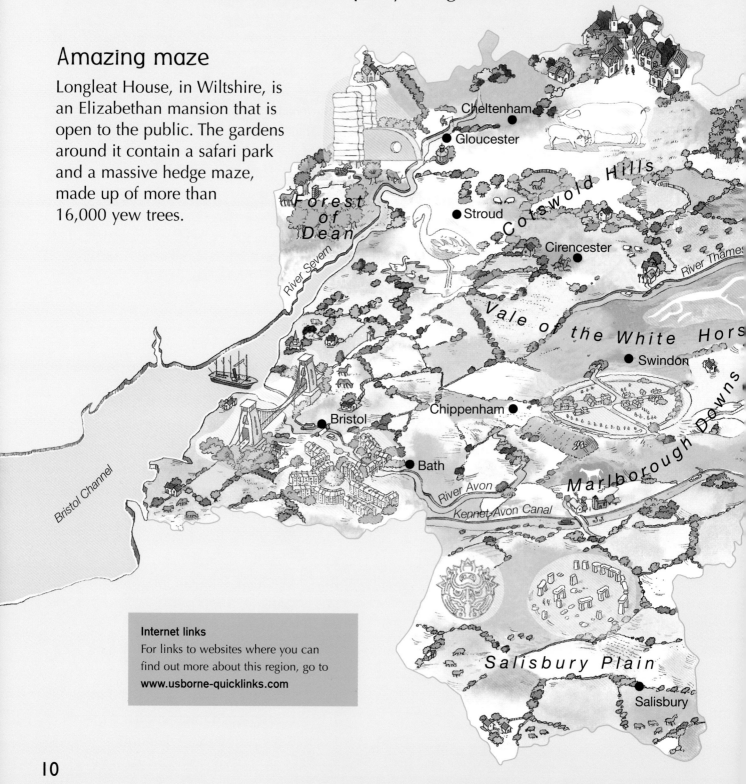

Cheltenham

Gloucester

Forest
of
Dean

River Severn

Stroud

Cotswold Hills

Cirencester

River Thames

Vale of the White Horse

Swindon

Marlborough Downs

Bristol

Chippenham

Bath

River Avon

Kennet-Avon Canal

Bristol Channel

Salisbury Plain

Salisbury

Internet links

For links to websites where you can
find out more about this region, go to
www.usborne-quicklinks.com

Chalk horse

The White Horse is a huge figure that was cut into a chalky hillside thousands of years ago. Some people believe that it shows an ancient horse god, while others think it may be a dragon.

Banbury

River Great Ouse

Bedford

Milton Keynes

Stevenage

Luton

Bishop's Stortford

Aylesbury

Oxford

St. Albans

Abingdon

Chiltern Hills

...shire Downs

High Wycombe

River Thames

Reading

Slough

River Kennet

Heart of England stickers

48 Sculpture Trail, Forest of Dean
49 Windsor Castle
50 Cotswold Farm Park, Stow-on-the-Wold
51 White Horse, Uffington
52 Whipsnade Wild Animal Park, Dunstable
53 Maypole dancing, Ickwell Green
54 Student, Oxford University
55 Clifton Suspension Bridge, Bristol
56 Stonehenge
57 Wildfowl and Wetlands Centre, Slimbridge
58 Maze, Longleat House, Warminster
59 Georgian houses, Bath
60 Hatfield House
61 Stone circle, Avebury
62 Bekonscot Model Village, Beaconsfield

Ancient stone circles

More than 5,000 years ago, many rings of stone pillars were constructed in the English countryside. Two of the most spectacular sites are Stonehenge and Avebury, where many of the stones still stand. No one is sure what the circles were for. They may have been ancient temples or burial sites.

East Anglia

East Anglia is the round part of eastern England that juts out into the North Sea. It is famous for its flat landscape, known as the Fens. This area was once marshland, but has now been drained, leaving rich soil, which is ideal for growing grain, fruit and vegetables.

Louth

Lincolnshire Wolds

Skegness

Lincoln

Boston

The Wash

King's Lynn

Grantham

Peterborough

Wisbech

The Fens

Ely

River Great Ouse

East Dereham

Norwich

River Yare

Norfolk Broads

Great Yarmouth

Lowestoft

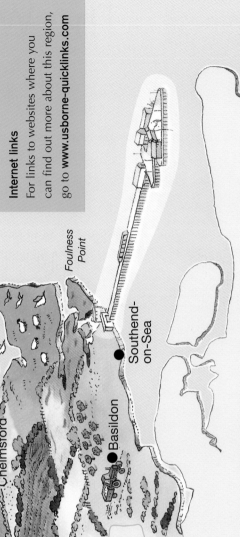

Sunken treasure

Some people believe that treasure belonging to King John of England lies at the bottom of a North Sea inlet called the Wash. In 1216, carts carrying all the king's jewels are said to have got stuck in quicksand near the Wash and then been swept away when the tide came in.

East Anglia stickers

Internet links

For links to websites where you can find out more about this region, go to **www.usborne-quicklinks.com**

A ship of jewels

In 1939, an archaeologist discovered graves of Anglo-Saxon kings at Sutton Hoo, near Woodbridge. All kinds of treasures had been buried with the kings, including an enormous boat filled with gold, silver and jewels.

Felixstowe

The Naze

Ipswich

River Stour

Harwich

Colchester

Clacton-on-Sea

Bury St. Edmunds

Chelmsford

Foulness Point

Southend-on-Sea

Basildon

Cambridge

Duxford

Harlow

The West Midlands

Internet links

For links to websites where you can find out more about this region, go to **www.usborne-quicklinks.com**

The Midlands make up central England, and the western part extends to the Welsh border. The area has a long history of making potter[y], china, chocolate and mar[y] other products.

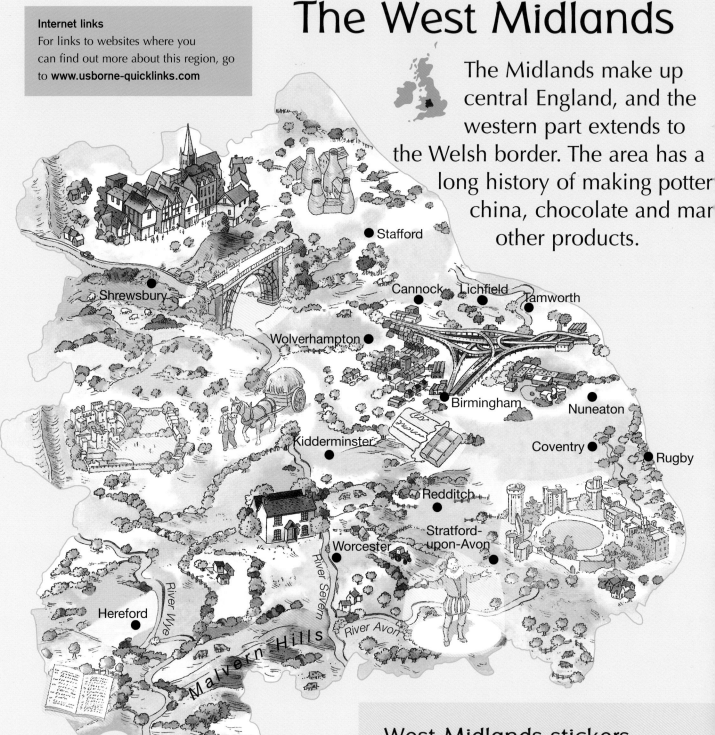

Stafford

Shrewsbury

Cannock   Lichfield   Tamworth

Wolverhampton

Kidderminster

Birmingham

Nuneaton

Coventry   Rugby

Redditch

Stratford-upon-Avon

Worcester

River Wye

River Severn

River Avon

Hereford

Malvern Hills

Shakespeare's home

The playwright William Shakespeare was born in the town of Stratford-upon-Avon in 1564. Thousands of visitors flock there every year to see the house where he was born, and to watch performances of his plays by the Royal Shakespeare Company.

West Midlands stickers

78   Acton Scott Historic Working Farm
79   Iron Bridge, Telford
80   Cadbury World, Bournville
81   Warwick Castle
82   Shakespearean play, Stratford-upon-Avon
83   Pottery factories
84   Book shops, Hay-on-Wye
85   Ludlow Castle

The East Midlands

The East Midlands have lots of scenic countryside, including the Peak District and Sherwood Forest.

Robin Hood

Robin Hood was a legendary outlaw and hero who is said to have lived in Sherwood Forest in the Middle Ages. Many stories are told of his daring adventures.

Deer dance

The village of Abbots Bromley has an annual event called the Horn Dance. It dates back to the thirteenth century and involves local men performing dances while carrying deer antlers.

East Midlands stickers

86   Alton Towers theme park

87   Robin Hood exhibition, Sherwood Forest

88   Butterfly and Aquatic Centre, Oakham

89   Heights of Abraham, Matlock Bath

90   Horn Dance, Abbots Bromley

91   Balloon festival, Northampton

92   Donington Park racetrack

93   Castleton Caverns

Internet links

For links to websites where you can find out more about this region, go to **www.usborne-quicklinks.com**

15

Northwest England

In the far northwest of England is the Lake District, a huge national park that contains beautiful lakes and mountains and is a popular place for walking, sailing and climbing trips. Further south are the busy cities of Liverpool and Manchester.

Beatrix Potter

Beatrix Potter wrote and illustrated famous stories about Peter Rabbit and other characters. She was born in 1866 in London, but she loved the Lake District and spent most of her time there.

Internet links

For links to websites where you can find out more about this region, go to www.usborne-quicklinks.com

Pennines

Penrith

Carlisle

Lake District

Kendal

Keswick

Scafell Pike

SOLWAY FIRTH

Workington

Whitehaven

St. Bees Head

Isle of Man

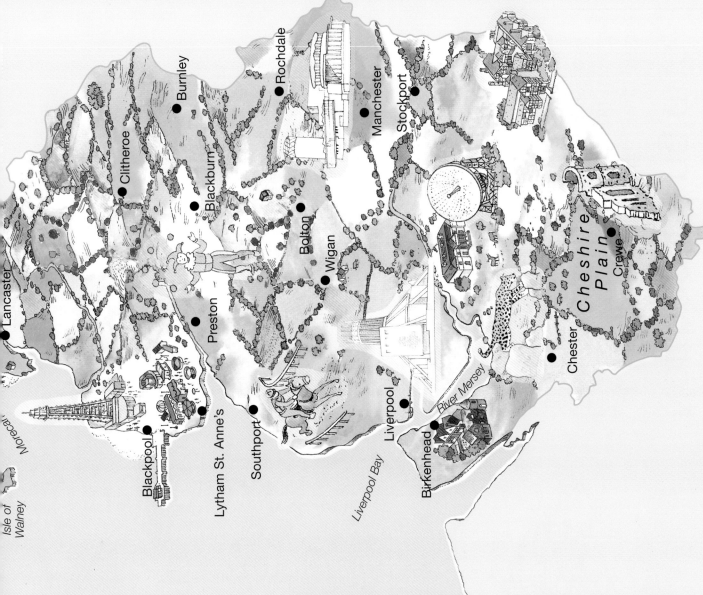

Isle of Walney

Morecambe

IRISH SEA

Lancaster

Clitheroe

Burnley

Blackburn

Rochdale

Manchester

Stockport

Preston

Bolton

Wigan

Blackpool

Lytham St. Anne's

Southport

Liverpool

Liverpool Bay

Birkenhead

River Mersey

Chester

Cheshire Plain

Crewe

Blackpool

Blackpool is one of Britain's busiest seaside resorts. It has a zoo, three piers, funfair rides and many other kinds of amusements. Its most famous building is Blackpool Tower, which was modelled on the Eiffel Tower, in Paris. It contains a ballroom, an aquarium and a circus.

Northwest England stickers

94   Lake Windermere
95   Camelot theme park, Chorley
96   Liverpool Metropolitan Cathedral
97   Little Moreton Hall, Congleton
98   Chester Zoo
99   Lady Isabella waterwheel
100 Lovell Telescope, Jodrell Bank
101 Hang-gliding, Lake District
102 Blackpool Tower
103 Cumberland and Westmorland wrestling
104 Mow Cop Castle
105 Beatrix Potter's home
106 Horseracing, Aintree racecourse
107 Cumberland Pencil Museum, Keswick
108 The Lowry, Salford

Northeast England

Northeast England has huge areas of rugged, windswept countryside. There are also many picturesque cities, including Durham and York.

Northeast England stickers

109 Trams, Beamish Open Air Museum
110 Lightwater Valley theme park
111 The Deep, Kingston upon Hull
112 Medieval fair, Alnwick
113 Ski Village, Sheffield
114 Holy Island (Lindisfarne)
115 York Minster
116 Angel of the North, Gateshead
117 National Museum of Photography, Film and Television, Bradford
118 Kielder Water
119 North Yorkshire Moors Railway
120 Cheese-making, Wensleydale
121 Humber Bridge
122 Hadrian's Wall
123 The Locomotion, Darlington Railway Museum
124 Jousting re-enactment, Royal Armouries Museum, Leeds

Internet links

For links to websites where you can find out more about this region, go to www.usborne-quicklinks.com

Berwick-upon-Tweed

Cheviot Hills

Ashington

Tynemouth

South Shields

Newcastle-upon-Tyne

Sunderland

Durham

Hartlepool

River Wear

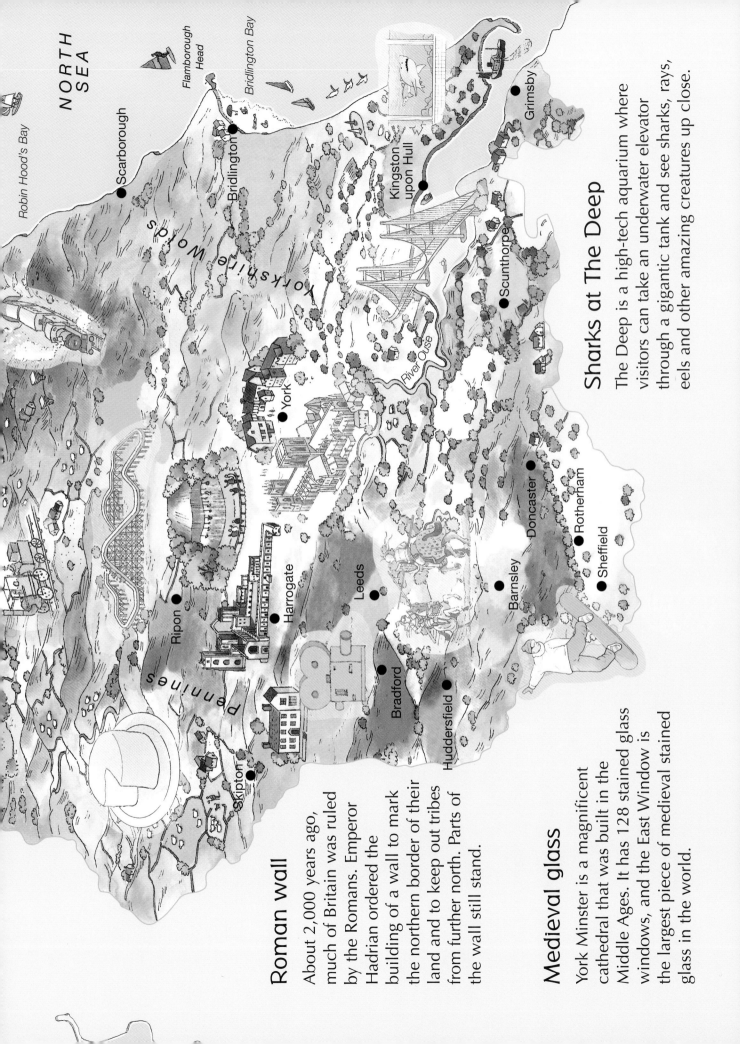

NORTH SEA

Robin Hood's Bay

Scarborough

Flamborough Head

Bridlington Bay

Bridlington

Yorkshire Wolds

Grimsby

Kingston upon Hull

Scunthorpe

River Ouse

York

Pennines

Ripon

Harrogate

Leeds

Doncaster

Rotherham

Sheffield

Barnsley

Skipton

Bradford

Huddersfield

Sharks at The Deep

The Deep is a high-tech aquarium where visitors can take an underwater elevator through a gigantic tank and see sharks, rays, eels and other amazing creatures up close.

Roman wall

About 2,000 years ago, much of Britain was ruled by the Romans. Emperor Hadrian ordered the building of a wall to mark the northern border of their land and to keep out tribes from further north. Parts of the wall still stand.

Medieval glass

York Minster is a magnificent cathedral that was built in the Middle Ages. It has 128 stained glass windows, and the East Window is the largest piece of medieval stained glass in the world.

Wales

Wales is a country of high mountains and deep valleys. Its capital is Cardiff, in the southeast. In the Middle Ages, Wales was often invaded by the English, and many big stone castles were built there.

Welsh festivals

Wales has a yearly arts festival called the Eisteddfod, which means "gathering" in Welsh. It is a week-long celebration of Welsh culture, and is held in a different place each year. There is also a musical Eisteddfod in Llangollen every July, where competitors from around the world take part in music, dance and song contests.

Going underground

Coal mining was once a vital industry in Wales. The Big Pit mine in Blaenafon shut in 1980 and is now a mining museum. Visitors go 90m (300ft) underground to learn what life was like for the many miners who used to dig for coal there.

Liverpool Bay

Flint

Rhyl

Llandudno

Great Ormes Head

Bangor

Anglesey

Holyhead

Holy Island

Caernarfon Bay

Braich y Pwll

Bardsey Island

Tremadog Bay

Pwllheli

Porthmadog

Blaenau Ffestiniog

Dolgellau

Welshpool

Newtown

Radnor Forest

Cambrian Mountains

Cardigan Bay

Aberystwyth

Aberaeron

Wales stickers

125 Museum of Welsh Life, St. Fagans
126 Erddig Hall, Wrexham ✓
127 National Cycle Exhibition,
     Llandrindod Wells
128 Millennium Stadium, Cardiff ✓
129 Caernarfon Castle ✓
130 Red kite, Cambrian Mountains ✓
131 International Music Eisteddfod, Llangollen
132 National Library of Wales, Aberystwyth ✓
133 Anglesey Sea Zoo ✓
134 Centre for Alternative Technology,
     Machynlleth
135 Grand Theatre, Swansea
136 Big Pit coal mine, Blaenafon
137 King Arthur's Labyrinth, Corris
138 Dinosaur Park, Abercrave
139 Tintern Abbey
140 National Woollen Museum, Llandysul

Internet links
For links to websites where you can
find out more about Wales, go to
www.usborne-quicklinks.com

Southern Scotland

Southern Scotland is known as the Lowlands, because it has fewer mountains than northern Scotland. Scotland's capital city, Edinburgh, is in the south, as is the country's biggest city, Glasgow.

A royal castle

Edinburgh Castle stands on an enormous rock, high above the city. The castle was the home of Scottish kings and is made up of many buildings, including a 12th-century chapel.

Internet links

For links to websites where you can find out more about this region, go to www.usborne-quicklinks.com

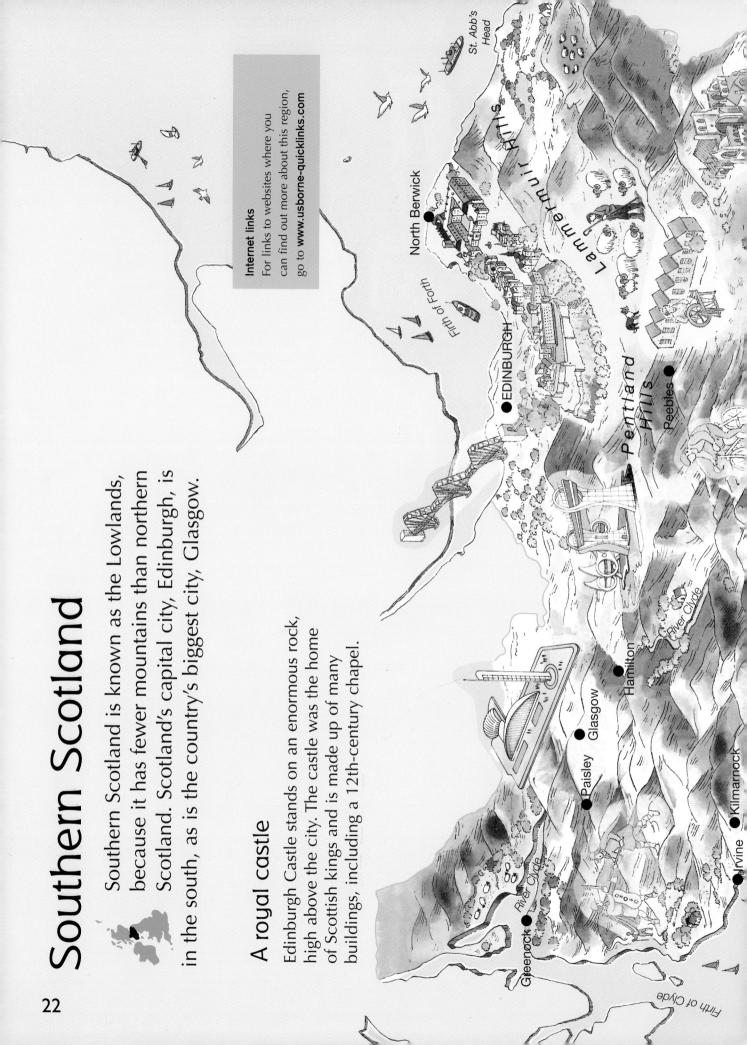

St. Abb's Head

North Berwick

Firth of Forth

Lammermuir Hills

EDINBURGH

Pentland Hills

Peebles

River Clyde

Hamilton

Glasgow

Paisley

Greenock

River Clyde

Kilmarnock

Irvine

Firth of Clyde

Southern Scotland stickers

141 Dolphins, Solway Firth
142 Forth Rail Bridge
143 Museum of Lead Mining, Wanlockhead
144 Glasgow Science Centre
145 Caerlaverock Castle
146 Edinburgh Castle
147 Melrose Abbey
148 Falkirk Wheel boat lift
149 Vikingar exhibition, Largs
150 Robert Burns statue, Dumfries
151 Wool mill, Galashiels
152 Fishing, Solway Firth
153 Blowplain Farm, Balmaclellan
154 Common Riding Festival, Selkirk
155 Mountain biking, Southern Uplands

Robert Burns

Scotland's best-known poet is Robert Burns. He was born in Alloway on 25 January 1759, and later lived in Dumfries. His birthday is remembered every year with a celebration called Burns Night.

Cheviot Hills

River Teviot

Moffat

Lockerbie

Southern Uplands

Dumfries

Solway Firth

Castle Douglas

Wigtown Bay

Mull of Galloway

Luce Bay

Girvan

Stranraer

Loch Ryan

23

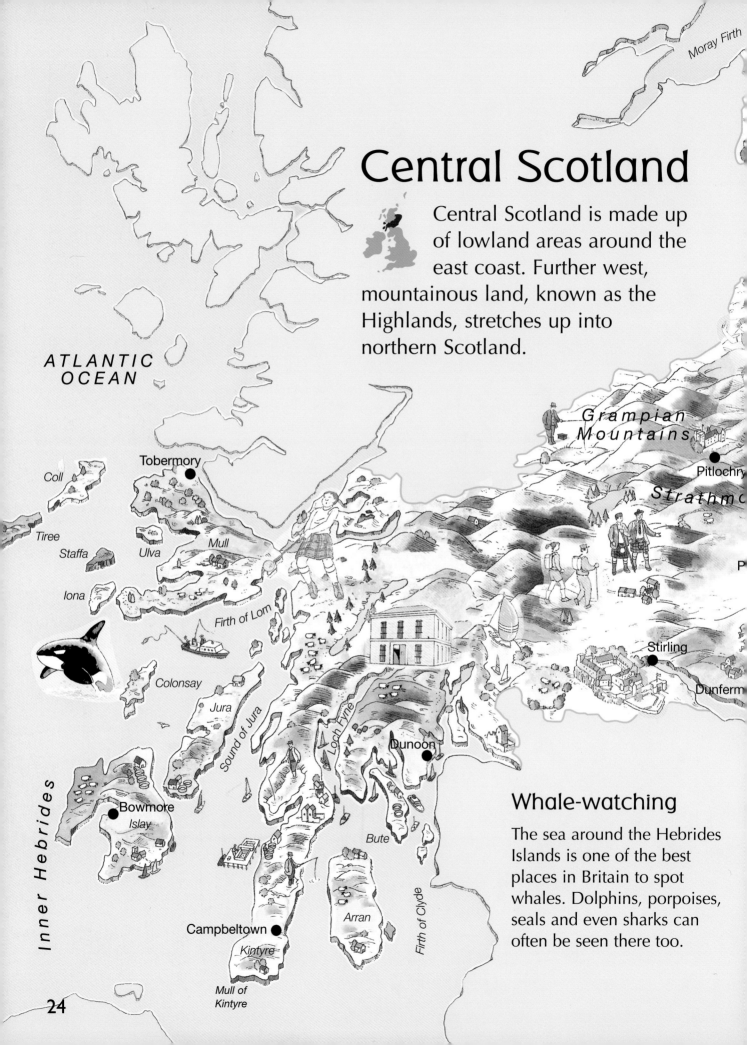

Central Scotland

Central Scotland is made up of lowland areas around the east coast. Further west, mountainous land, known as the Highlands, stretches up into northern Scotland.

Moray Firth

ATLANTIC OCEAN

Grampian Mountains

Pitlochry

Strathm

Tobermory

Coll

Tiree

Staffa

Ulva

Mull

Iona

Firth of Lom

Colonsay

Jura

Sound of Jura

Loch Fyne

Dunoon

Stirling

Dunferm

Bowmore

Islay

Inner Hebrides

Bute

Firth of Clyde

Arran

Campbeltown

Kintyre

Mull of Kintyre

Whale-watching

The sea around the Hebrides Islands is one of the best places in Britain to spot whales. Dolphins, porpoises, seals and even sharks can often be seen there too.

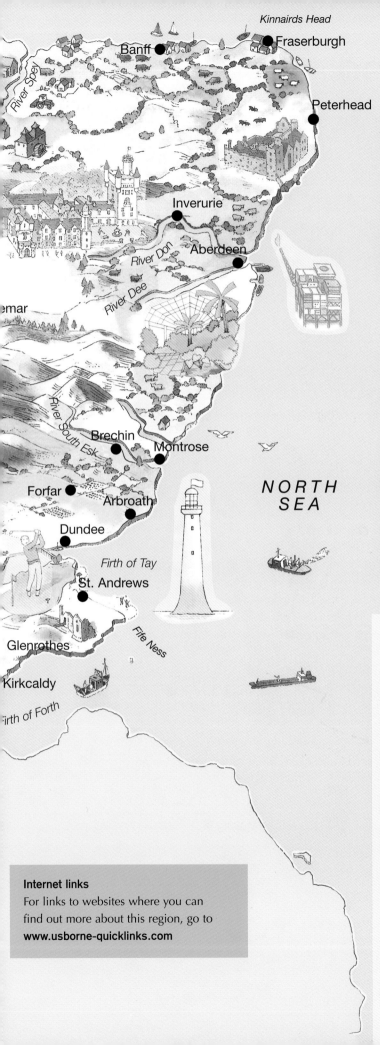

Traditional sports

The Highland Games are displays of traditional Scottish sports, dance and music, and are held in towns throughout Scotland every summer. Events such as throwing heavy weights or tossing the caber, a huge, trimmed tree trunk, require a lot of strength.

Creepy castle

Slains Castle stands on a jagged cliff edge on the North Sea coast. It was built in 1597 and is now in ruins. The author Bram Stoker visited the castle in 1895, and might have used it in his novel *Dracula* as the model for Dracula's spooky home.

Central Scotland stickers

156	Throwing the weight, Highland Games, Oban
157	Slains Castle, Cruden Bay
158	Balmoral Castle
159	Walking, the Trossachs
160	Killer whale, Hebrides Sea
161	Golfing, St. Andrews
162	Oil platform, North Sea
163	Inveraray Jail
164	Duthie Park Winter Gardens, Aberdeen
165	Highland dancing
166	Loch Lomond
167	Stirling Castle
168	Bell Rock Lighthouse

Internet links
For links to websites where you can find out more about this region, go to www.usborne-quicklinks.com

Northern Scotland

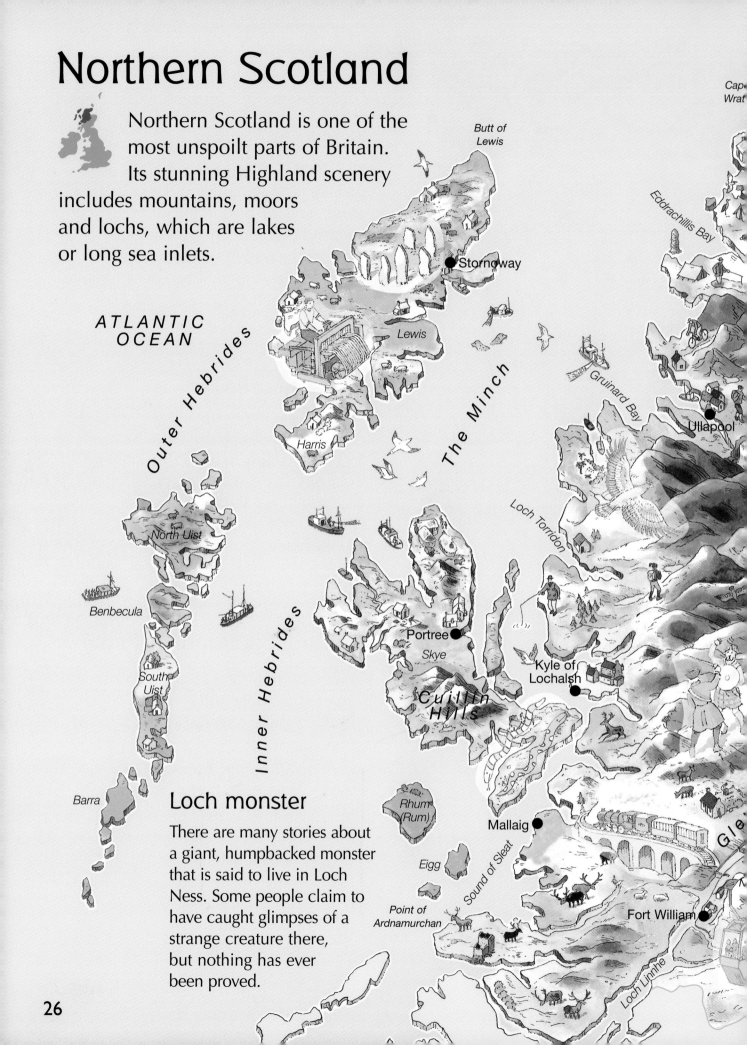

Northern Scotland is one of the most unspoilt parts of Britain. Its stunning Highland scenery includes mountains, moors and lochs, which are lakes or long sea inlets.

ATLANTIC OCEAN

Outer Hebrides

Inner Hebrides

The Minch

Butt of Lewis

Cap
Wrat

Eddrachillis Bay

●Stornoway

Lewis

Harris

Gruinard Bay

●Ullapool

North Uist

Benbecula

South Uist

Loch Torridon

Barra

Portree●

Skye

Cuillin Hills

Kyle of Lochalsh●

Loch monster

There are many stories about a giant, humpbacked monster that is said to live in Loch Ness. Some people claim to have caught glimpses of a strange creature there, but nothing has ever been proved.

Rhum (Rum)

Eigg

Point of Ardnamurchan

Mallaig●

Sound of Sleat

Gle

Fort William●

Loch Linnhe

To the Shetland Islands ↗

Northern islands

The Orkney Islands are a group of scenic islands just off the northeast tip of mainland Scotland. Further north still are the rugged, windswept Shetland Islands, the most northerly part of Britain.

High ride

Britain's highest mountain, Ben Nevis, is 1,343m (4,406ft) high. You can get good views of it by taking a cable car up a nearby mountain called Aonach Mor.

Northern Scotland stickers

Internet links
For links to websites where you can find out more about this region, go to
www.usborne-quicklinks.com

Northern Ireland

Northern Ireland's varied landscape includes mountains, farmland and lakes called loughs. Its capital is Belfast, a large city which is home to around a sixth of the country's population.

Internet links
For links to websites where you can find out more about Northern Ireland, go to
www.usborne-quicklinks.com

Ireland's saint

On March 17th, Irish people celebrate St. Patrick's Day. St. Patrick was a famous fifth-century bishop who is buried in Downpatrick.

Belfast cranes

Samson and Goliath are two towering cranes that belong to a shipbuilding company. They dominate the Belfast skyline and are well-known symbols of Belfast's long history of shipbuilding.

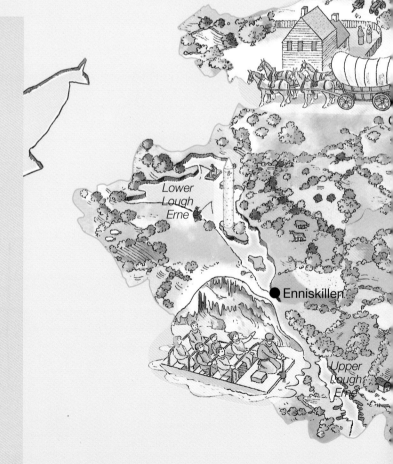

Londonde (Derry)

Str

Lower Lough Erne

Enniskillen

Upper Lough Erne

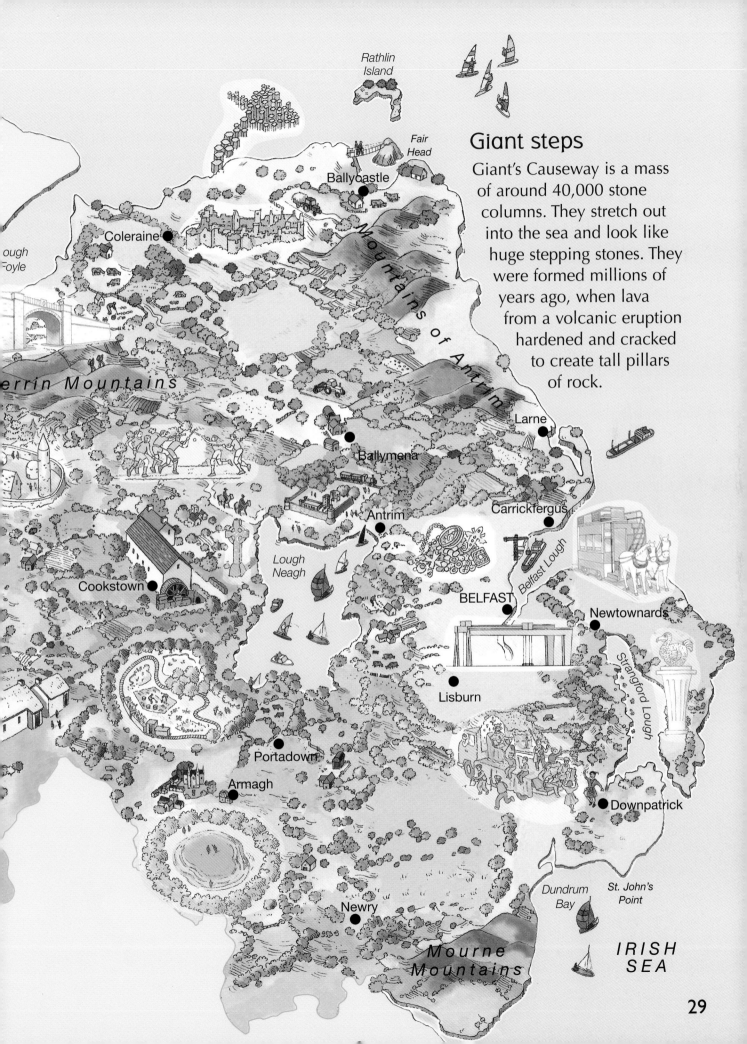

Rathlin Island

Fair Head

Ballycastle

Coleraine

Lough Foyle

Mountains of Antrim

errin Mountains

Larne

Ballymena

Antrim

Carrickfergus

Belfast Lough

Cookstown

Lough Neagh

BELFAST

Newtownards

Lisburn

Strangford Lough

Portadown

Armagh

Downpatrick

Newry

Dundrum Bay

St. John's Point

Mourne Mountains

IRISH SEA

Giant steps

Giant's Causeway is a mass of around 40,000 stone columns. They stretch out into the sea and look like huge stepping stones. They were formed millions of years ago, when lava from a volcanic eruption hardened and cracked to create tall pillars of rock.

Quiz questions

On the next few pages you'll find more than 200 quiz questions about Great Britain and Northern Ireland. Look back through the maps in this book to help you answer them. You'll find all the answers on pages 44-45.

1. Which country's flag is NOT included in the design of the Union Flag?

2. In which lake or loch is there said to be a monster?
a. Lake Windermere
b. Loch Lomond
c. Loch Ness

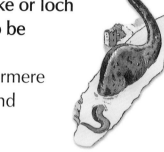

3. What is the name of the narrow body of water between the south coast of England and the Isle of Wight?

4. Which islands are the most northerly in the UK?
a. Orkney Isles
b. Shetland Isles
c. Isles of Scilly

5. What is the name of this structure, built in England to keep out tribes from the far north?

6. What is the East Anglian network of rivers and lakes that you can sail along in Norfolk called?
a. the wides
b. the narrows
c. the broads

7. Where could you find an art gallery named after the English artist L.S. Lowry, who was famous for painting industrial scenes in northwest England?

8. When does the town of Ottery St. Mary, in the southwest, hold a festival involving barrels of burning tar?
a. October 31st
b. November 5th
c. December 25th

9. What is the name of the highest mountain in Britain?
a. Snowdon
b. Scafell Pike
c. Ben Nevis

10. Which river flows through the heart of London?

11. Which of these is NOT part of the United Kingdom?
a. Isle of Man
b. Isle of Wight
c. Western Isles

12. Where can you visit the Giant's Causeway?
a. Wales
b. Scotland
c. Northern Ireland

13. Which Scottish city is furthest north: Inverness or Dundee?

14. What is the name of this famous warship that's moored in Portsmouth?

15. Where is this column erected in tribute to the admiral, Horatio Nelson, whose flagship is in question 14?

16. Which of these is the name of a group of sharp rocks in the Atlantic Ocean, just off the coast of England?
a. the pins   b. the needles   c. the spikes

17. Where do the yacht races during Cowes Week take place?

18. Which body of water separates Wales from the island of Anglesey?

19. Who is the famous playwright who was born in Stratford-upon-Avon: William Shakespeare or Robert Burns?

20. What could you do at Aviemore in Scotland?
a. swim with sharks
b. go skiing
c. go windsurfing

21. In which seaside town would you find this tower, modelled on the Eiffel Tower in Paris?

22. Britain is the largest island in Europe. True or false?

23. What's the name of the bay that Aberystwyth overlooks?
a. Cardigan Bay
b. Jersey Bay
c. Coat Bay

24. On which island could you find the Lady Isabella waterwheel?

25. The name of the most southerly point in mainland England shares its name with which type of animal?
a. lizard   b. penguin   c. otter

26. Where in the north of Britain are the Grampian Mountains?
a. Southern Scotland
b. Central Scotland
c. Northern Scotland

27. What is the name of the area in London famous for this parade?
a. Thaitown
b. Chinatown
c. Japantown

28. Match each flag to the correct saint, and the country it represents:

St. Patrick   St. George   St. Andrew

Scotland   Northern Ireland   England

29. In which northern city could you visit the National Museum of Photography, Film and Television?
a. Leeds   b. Bradford   c. York

30. What's the name of this ancient landmark that stands in the middle of Salisbury Plain?

31. Coll, Iona and Mull are all in which island group?

32. Which sea around the UK is known for its many oil platforms?
a. North Sea
b. Irish Sea
c. Hebrides Sea

33. In which northern city could you watch a jousting re-enactment at the Royal Armouries Museum?

34. Where in the Midlands does a balloon festival take place?

35. In which forest could you follow a famous sculpture trail: The New Forest or The Forest of Dean?

36. What are lakes called in Northern Ireland?
a. lochs   b. loughs   c. lagoons

37. Which royal residence is this, that lies just west of Slough, in the heart of England?

38. In 1066, a famous battle for the English throne was fought at Hastings. Which coast is it on?
a. south coast
b. east coast
c. west coast

39. Which London cathedral has one of the highest domed roofs in the world?

40. Which northern city would you find near the mouth of the River Tees?
a. Grimsby
b. Middlesbrough
c. Kingston upon Hull

41. What is the northeastern town of Wensleydale famous for?

42. Welshpool is not in Wales.
True or false?

43. This bridge over the River Severn was the first arch bridge in the world to be made from which material?

a. Cast Iron
b. Concrete
c. Steel

44. Roughly how many people live in the United Kingdom?
a. 40 million
b. 60 million
c. 80 million

45. Which museum could you visit in the north to see lots of trams like these?
a. Museum of Welsh Life
b. Darlington Railway Museum
c. Beamish Open Air Museum

46. What is the name of the city just north of Loch Ness?
a. Inverness
b. Lockerbie
c. Skegness

47. With which country is the sport of hurling, being played in the picture below, associated?

48. Where is the Peak District?
a. The Midlands
b. Southeast England
c. Northwest England

49. What unusual kind of museum is there at Keswick in the Lake District?

50. In which city could you see this cathedral?
a. Lincoln
b. Exeter
c. Canterbury

51. What does the London store Hamleys sell?
a. toys   b. pets   c. meat

52. When did Northern Ireland first become a part of the United Kingdom?
a. 1606   b. 1653   c. 1801

53. What kind of mines is Wales particularly known for, such as the Big Pit in Blaenafon, north of Cardiff?
a. lead mines
b. coal mines
c. flint mines

54. Which south coast town has 'Royal' at the start of its name?
a. Winchester
b. Eastbourne
c. Tunbridge Wells

55. It's said that this castle, whose ruins stand on the North Sea coast, could have inspired Dracula's castle. What is its name?

56. Which point is directly west of John o' Groats, on the opposite coast of the Scottish mainland?

57. Where in the heart of England could you walk around the model village that is pictured on the right?

58. In which town is St. Patrick buried?
a. Coleraine
b. Ballymena
c. Downpatrick

59. Where could you visit the National Library of Wales, pictured below?

60. What scientific instrument could you find at Jodrell Bank, southwest of Manchester?

61. Which of these West Country areas lies furthest north?
a. Bodmin Moor
b. Dartmoor
c. Exmoor

62. Melrose abbey is a little north of which town in southern Scotland?

63. Which building, the heart of the UK government, is this clocktower a part of?
a. Buckingham Palace
b. Houses of Parliament
c. Tower of London

64. Where is the marshy region known as the Fens?
a. East Anglia
b. Northeast England
c. Southern Scotland

65. What do these Midlands factories north of Stafford produce?

66. What is the most westerly point of mainland England?

67. With which sport is the south coast village of Hambledon most famously associated?
a. cricket   b. rugby   c. tennis

68. Which ruined castle overlooks the Atlantic Ocean and is said to be built on the spot where King Arthur was born?
a. Dover Castle
b. Tintagel Castle
c. Warwick Castle

69. Which of these places does NOT lie on the River Severn?
a. Gloucester
b. Shrewsbury
c. Hereford

70. This statue stands in which city in memory of Robert Burns, Scotland's most famous poet?

71. What is the name of the body of water between Lewis and the Scottish mainland?
a. The Minch
b. The Wash
c. Menai Strait

72. Greenock in southern Scotland is on the banks of which river?

73. Where is the horse below cut into a chalky English hillside?

74. What do some people think the horse could be?

a. a unicorn
b. a dragon
c. a minotaur

75. Where in the Midlands has this annual horn dance taken place since the thirteenth century?

76. Who runs the UK as the head of the government?
a. the President
b. the Queen
c. the Prime Minister

77. What's the name of the range of hills a little way north of Hadrian's Wall?

78. This castle lies just east of Inverness. What is its name?

79. What natural event created the Giant's Causeway?
a. earthquake
b. tidal wave
c. volcanic eruption

80. Where did Beatrix Potter, who created Peter Rabbit, spend most of her time?

81. Does the River Thames flow through London: west to east or north to south?

82. What is the Union Flag, pictured below, more commonly known as?

83. What is the function of this Scottish building?
a. museum
b. science centre
c. parliament building

84. What, in Northern Ireland, are Samson and Goliath?

85. Where on the south coast would you find the Royal Pavilion?

86. Which northern river is Durham on?
a. Derwent   b. Wear   c. Tyne

87. Which theme park is pictured below, located north of Ripon?

88. Aintree is a famous racecourse that lies in the north of which city?
a. Manchester
b. Liverpool
c. Lancaster

89. Kielder Water, the largest artificial lake in the UK, is south of Hadrian's Wall. True or false?

90. The town of Stranraer is close to which Scottish loch?

91. What is this device, and where in the north of Britain would you be able to find it?

92. Which saint is the crown that kings and queens of England wear named after?

93. The Eisteddfod is a yearly arts festival in which country?
a. Wales
b. Scotland
c. Northern Ireland

94. What is the name of this piece of land near Land's End?
a. St. Michael's Mount
b. Lundy Island
c. Lindisfarne

95. Which capital city is furthest north in the United Kingdom?
a. Belfast   b. Cardiff   c. Edinburgh

96. In which elevated region could you explore the Castleton Caverns?
a. Peak District
b. Lake District
c. Mendip Hills

97. Which London museum's dinosaur exhibits include a huge 26m (85ft) long Diplodocus skeleton?

98. Which of these mountain ranges in Northern Ireland is furthest south?
a. Mountains of Antrim
b. Mourne Mountains
c. Sperrin Mountains

99. Which historical period are these houses in Bath from?
a. Georgian
b. Edwardian
c. Victorian

100. Scafell Pike, the highest mountain in England, is in which region?
a. Highlands
b. Peak District
c. Lake District

101. Which hills in the Midlands lie between the River Wye and the River Severn?

102. Which warship is this, moored on the Thames, and now used as a museum ship by the Imperial War Museum?

103. Londonderry in Northern Ireland lies on which river?

104. Which royal residence, situated west of Aberdeen, is pictured below?

105. What attraction could you find in Beaulieu, near Southampton?

106. Which of these is furthest north?
a. Firth of Lorn
b. Firth of Tay
c. Moray Firth

107. In which northern cathedral could you find the largest piece of medieval stained glass in the world?

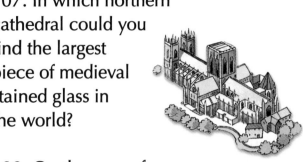

108. On the map of Northern Ireland, Lower Lough Erne is above Upper Lough Erne. True or false?

109. Which islands lie just off the northeast tip of Scotland?
a. Isles of Scilly
b. Orkney Islands
c. Inner Hebrides

110. Corris in Wales is home to an exhibition related to which king of British legend?

111. Which is a real place on the coast of East Anglia: Foulness Point or Vileness Head?

112. What type of building is this in Liverpool?
a. cathedral
b. museum
c. factory

113. What is the name of this huge winged sculpture you could see as you head north past Gateshead?

114. What is the largest natural lake in England, found in the Lake District?

115. Which island in the north of England is also known as Holy Island?

116. Which major airport lies south of London, near Reigate?

117. Which northern range of hills lies southeast of Carlisle?
a. Pennines
b. Chiltern Hills
c. Cotswold Hills

118. The castle below stands in which capital city in the United Kingdom?

119. Which of these is NOT a point on the south coast?
a. Bill of Portland
b. Selsey Bill
c. St. Catherine's Bill

120. What is Dartmoor in the West Country more famous for:
deer or ponies?

121. In which English region would you find the ruins of Glastonbury Abbey?

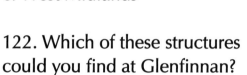

a. West Country
b. East Anglia
c. West Midlands

122. Which of these structures could you find at Glenfinnan?
a. dam
b. viaduct
c. suspension bridge

123. Throwing the weight is one of the events in which traditional Scottish sporting display?

124. What kind of mine is at Thetford, southwest of Norwich?
a. flint mine
b. gold mine
c. tin mine

125. What kind of museum could you find in Colchester in East Anglia?

126. Mount Stewart House, in Northern Ireland, has a terrace named after which bird?
a. puffin
b. dodo
c. tern

127. Which restored London building puts on Shakespeare's plays as they would have been shown in his own time?

128. Where are the Marble Arch caves?
a. Central London
b. Northern Ireland
c. Southern Scotland

129. Where can you find the Eden Project's giant domed greenhouses?
a. The West Country
b. The South Coast
c. East Anglia

130. Where could you see dolphins, a little way south of Dumfries?

131. What was discovered at Sutton Hoo in East Anglia in 1939?

132. Which mountain's cable cars give a good view of Ben Nevis?

133. On which river is the Midlands town of Derby?
a. Derwent   b. Wye   c. Avon

134. In which city could you visit the Millennium Stadium?

135. In which northern nature reserve could you see golden eagles like this one?

136. Roughly how many people live in London?
a. 3 million   b. 9 million   c. 15 million

137. Which suspension bridge spans the large estuary just west of Kingston upon Hull?

138. Which city is located just west of the mouth of the Firth of Forth?
a. Dundee   b. Stirling   c. Aberdeen

139. Leeds Castle is in the northern city of Leeds.
True or false?

140. What is the name of the National Park that Brecon is on the northern border of?

141. Which type of trees are there more than 16,000 of in the maze at Longleat House in the heart of England?

142. Which famous East Anglian university is this building a part of?

143. The Queen of the UK is elected. True or false?

144. When is Burns Night celebrated: November 5th **or** January 25th?

145. What's the name of this enormous wheel on the South Bank that offers spectacular views of London?

146. Which of these is NOT the name of a place in Wales?
a. Newtown
b. Newport
c. Newquay

147. What is the name of the country house below, just south of Stevenage?

148. What kind of shops is the English town of Hay-on-Wye, near the Welsh border, particularly famous for?

149. In which direction is Glasgow from Edinburgh?

150. The capital of Wales lies on which body of water?
a. The Humber Estuary
b. The Bristol Channel
c. Swansea Bay

151. Where can you go to see how chocolate is made near Birmingham?

152. Where in the northeast could you go to see a medieval fair?

153. What, in northeast England, is The Deep: a high-tech aquarium **or** Britain's deepest lake?

154. Which island monastery stands in the middle of Lower Lough Erne?

155. In which east coast inlet do some people think King John's treasure lies?

156. Llandrindod Wells is close to which two mountain ranges?

157. Where would you find the Cotswold Hills?
a. The West Country
b. The Heart of England
c. Northeast England

158. Which North Sea lighthouse is this, standing east of the Firth of Tay?

159. What is the capital of the Isle of Man?

160. The city of Liverpool is on which river?
a. Mersey   b. Ouse   c. Teviot

161. Where could you visit a museum to see treasure from the Spanish Armada?
a. Cardiff
b. Belfast
c. Edinburgh

162. Tower Bridge is named after which nearby landmark on the north bank of the Thames?

163. Which of these south coast towns is famous for a long pier, full of amusement arcades?
a. Southampton
b. Folkestone
c. Brighton

164. What is the name of the range of hills on the isle of Skye?

165. Which old jail is this, offering magnificent views out over Loch Fyne?

166. Which of these could you NOT find inside Blackpool tower?
a. circus
b. aquarium
c. planetarium

167. Which southern town near Basingstoke hosts an international airshow every other year?

168. In which two counties in northwest England could you see traditional wrestling?

169. Where in northeast Scotland might you pan for gold?

170. Which seaside town is just south of the Bedruthan Steps?
a. Newquay
b. Blackpool
c. Great Yarmouth

171. What's the name of this theme park, east of Stoke-on-Trent?

172. Which town in the northeast is the most northerly town in England?

173. Which of these rivers flows into the Bristol Channel?
a. Great Ouse   b. Severn   c. Thames

174. Which famous golf course lies on the North Sea coast?

175. In which country is Tintern Abbey?
a. Wales
b. Scotland
c. England

176. What takes place every year on Ickwell Green near Bedford, in the heart of England?

177. Which London park has a famous boating lake?

178. Which island lies northeast of the Giant's Causeway?

179. The Museum of Lead Mining is in which country?
a. Wales
b. Scotland
c. Northern Ireland

180. On which coast of England is Sunderland?
a. south coast
b. west coast
c. east coast

181. Which of these is a real inlet in Scotland: Hairville Bay or Wigtown Bay?

182. Where is the tallest stone cross in Northern Ireland, dating from the tenth century?

183. What is the name of this infamous prison in London?

184. Which of these places in East Anglia is furthest south?
a. Harwich   b. Ipswich   c. Norwich

185. What is the name of this bridge that crosses the River Avon at Bristol?

186. Which hills lie east of Edinburgh: Pentland Hills or Lammermuir Hills?

187. Where off the northeast coast of Scotland might you see divers in search of shipwrecks?

188. Which of these points on the Welsh coast is furthest south?
a. St. David's Head
b. Strumble Head
c. Holyhead

189. Robin Hood's legendary home, Sherwood Forest, is just north of which city?

190. Which city lies just to the west of the mouth of the Firth of Tay?
a. Dunfermline
b. Kilmarnock
c. Perth

191. What is the name of this West Country tin mine near Falmouth?

192. The sea around which islands is a good place to spot whales?
a. The Hebrides
b. Isles of Scilly
c. Shetland Islands

193. Where in Wales could you visit the Dinosaur Park?

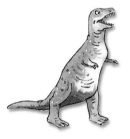

194. In which hills in the West Country would you find Wookey Hole Caves?
a. Mendip Hills
b. Chiltern Hills
c. Malvern Hills

195. Which bridge in southern Scotland crosses the Firth of Forth just west of Edinburgh?

196. Where is the Ulster American Folk Park, pictured below?

197. Which island in the Hebrides is the furthest north?
a. Skye   b. Lewis   c. Jura

198. Which mythical creature appears on the national flag of Wales?
a. centaur   b. griffin   c. dragon

199. Where in East Anglia could you visit the Imperial War Museum and see Spitfires like this one?

200. From which port town on the south coast can you catch an underwater train through the Channel Tunnel to France?
a. Newhaven
b. Bournemouth
c. Folkestone

201. Which university, the oldest in the UK, is on the River Thames?
a. Oxford
b. Cambridge
c. Durham

202. The River Severn is joined by which other river just south of Worcester?
a. Wye   b. Avon   c. Kennet

203. Which of these is a real place on the northwest coast of England: St. Bees Head or St. Wasps Head?

204. What particular type of dancing might you associate with the East Anglian town of Thaxted?

205. Which London building is protected by guards dressed in uniforms like the one on the right?

Quiz Answers

Page 30:

1. Wales 2. c 3. The Solent 4. b 5. Hadrian's Wall 6. c 7. Salford 8. b (Bonfire Night) 9. c 10. River Thames 11. a 12. c

Page 31:

13. Inverness 14. HMS Victory 15. London (Nelson's Column stands in Trafalgar Square, which is named after the famous sea battle in which he defeated the combined French and Spanish fleets, and in which he was killed.) 16. b 17. In the sea around the Isle of Wight 18. The Menai Strait 19. William Shakespeare 20. b 21. Blackpool (It was opened in 1894, five years after the Eiffel tower.) 22. True 23. a 24. Isle of Man 25. a 26. b 27. b

Page 32:

28. St. George, England

 St. Andrew, Scotland

 St. Patrick, Northern Ireland

29. b 30. Stonehenge 31. Inner Hebrides 32. a 33. Leeds 34. Northampton 35. The Forest of Dean 36. b 37. Windsor Castle 38. a 39. St. Paul's Cathedral (Designed by Sir Christopher Wren, it was the tallest building in London from 1710 to 1962.) 40. b 41. Cheese (Wensleydale is famously a favourite cheese of Wallace in the animated series *Wallace and Gromit*.) 42. False

Page 33:

43. a 44. b 45. c 46. a 47. Northern Ireland 48. a 49. Pencil Museum 50. b 51. a 52. c

Page 34:

53. b 54. c (It is one of just three English towns with the title, which was bestowed upon it by King Edward VII in 1909.) 55. Slains Castle

56. Cape Wrath 57. Beaconsfield (Bekonscot is the world's oldest original model village.) 58. c (The name comes from the Irish for 'Patrick's stronghold'.) 59. Aberystwyth 60. Lovell Telescope 61. c 62. Jedburgh 63. b (It is called the Elizabeth Tower, but it is generally known as Big Ben after the name of the bell inside it.) 64. a 65. Pottery 66. Land's End 67. a 68. b 69. c

Page 35:

70. Dumfries 71. a 72. River Clyde 73. Uffington 74. b 75. Abbots Bromley 76. c 77. Cheviot Hill 78. Cawdor Castle (Cawdor is famously associated with Shakespeare's Macbeth, who was Thane of Cawdor, but the play is not historically accurate and the castle was built centuries after the real Scottish king Macbeth.) 79. c 80. The Lake District 81. West to east 82. Union Jack 83. b

Page 36:

84. Huge shipbuilding gantry cranes in Belfast 85. Brighton (It was built as a royal retreat for the Prince of Wales, who later became George IV.) 86. b 87. Lightwater Valley theme park 88. b 89. False 90. Loch Ryan in southern Scotland 91. Falkirk Wheel boat lift, near Falkirk (It is the only rotating boat lift of its kind in the world.) 92. St. Edward (It is named after the king Edward the Confessor, who later became a saint, although the original crown was destroyed by Oliver Cromwell after the English Civil War.) 93. a 94. a 95. c 96. a 97. The Natural History Museum 98. b

Quiz Answers

Page 37:

99. a **100.** c **101.** Malvern Hills **102.** HMS Belfast **103.** River Foyle **104.** Balmoral Castle **105.** National Motor Museum **106.** c **107.** York Minster **108.** True **109.** b **110.** King Arthur **111.** Foulness Point **112.** a

Page 38:

113. The Angel of the North **114.** Lake Windermere **115.** Lindisfarne **116.** Gatwick airport (It is the second biggest international airport in the UK after Heathrow.) **117.** a **118.** Edinburgh **119.** c (although there is a St Catherine's Point) **120.** ponies **121.** a **122.** b **123.** The Highland Games **124.** a **125.** A Clock Museum **126.** b

Page 39:

127. The Globe Theatre **128.** b **129.** a **130.** Solway Firth **131.** An Anglo-Saxon royal burial site, including a ship full of jewels **132.** Aonach Mor **133.** a **134.** Cardiff **135.** Beinn Eighe nature reserve **136.** b **137.** Humber Bridge **138.** b **139.** False (It is named after a nearby village in Kent, also called Leeds.) **140.** The Brecon Beacons **141.** Yew trees **142.** Cambridge University (It is the second-oldest university in the UK.) **143.** False

Page 40:

144. January 25th (Robert Burns's birthday) **145.** The London Eye **146.** c **147.** Hatfield House **148.** Book shops **149.** West **150.** b **151.** Cadbury World, Bournville **152.** Alnwick **153.** A high-tech aquarium **154.** Devenish Monastery **155.** The Wash **156.** The Black Mountains and the Cambrian Mountains **157.** b

158. Bell Rock Lighthouse (It was built by Robert Stevenson, grandfather of the famous author Robert Louis Stevenson.) **159.** Douglas **160.** a

Page 41:

161. b **162.** The Tower of London **163.** c **164.** Cuillin Hills **165.** Inveraray Jail **166.** c **167.** Farnborough **168.** Cumberland and Westmorland **169.** Baile an Or **170.** a **171.** Alton Towers **172.** Berwick-upon-Tweed **173.** b **174.** St. Andrews (It's known worldwide as 'the home of golf'.) **175.** a **176.** Maypole dancing

Page 42:

177. Hyde Park **178.** Rathlin Island **179.** b **180.** c **181.** Wigtown Bay **182.** Ardboe **183.** The Tower of London (Its primary purpose was as a royal residence, but it has become more famous for its function as a prison, which it was used for as recently as 1952.) **184.** a **185.** Clifton Suspension Bridge **186.** Lammermuir Hills **187.** Pentland Firth **188.** a **189.** Nottingham (The Sheriff of Nottingham is the main villain in the legend of Robin Hood.) **190.** c **191.** Poldark Mine

Page 43:

192. a **193.** Abercrave **194.** a **195.** Forth Rail Bridge **196.** Omagh, Northern Ireland **197.** b **198.** c **199.** Duxford **200.** c **201.** a **202.** b **203.** St. Bees Head **204.** Morris dancing (Thaxted's is the oldest revival Morris dancing group in the country.) **205.** Buckingham Palace (The Queen's Guard, as they are known, guard all of the royal residences in the UK, but are most famously associated with Buckingham Palace, the official royal palace.)

Index and checklist

This checklist will help you to find where the stickers go. The first number after each entry tells you which page the sticker is on. The second number is the number next to the sticker.

Edited by Gillian Doherty and Louie Stowell
Cartographic editor: Craig Asquith
Consultants: Dr. Gillian McIntosh, Queen's University Belfast;
Dr. James Oliver, University of Edinburgh;
Dr. Paul Readman, King's College London;
Dr. Steven Thompson, University of Wales, Aberystwyth
With thanks to Fiona Patchett and Alice Pearcey
Cover design by Stephen Moncrieff and Sam Chandler
Digital manipulation by Katie Mayes, Mike Olley
and Nick Wakeford